This book belongs to:

Given with love by:

A Wish for the Water

Little one,
you are loved more than you can imagine.
And as you grow, explore, splash, and discover the water,
may you always have someone beside you—
watching closely,
guiding gently,
and helping you learn with calm, confidence, and joy.

The water will be part of your life.
And we hope every moment you spend in it
is safe, supported, and full of wonder.

You are cherished.
You are protected.
And you'll never face the water alone.

© 2025 Michael Godleski. All rights reserved.

ISBN: 979-8-9939476-0-0
Imprint: Prepare2Swim Publishing

Prepare2Swim™ is a trademark of Michael Godleski.

No part of this publication may be reproduced, stored in a retrieval system, or transmitted in any form or by any means without prior written permission from the publisher, except for brief quotations in reviews.

Gentle Safety Reminder
This book is designed to help parents introduce children to water in a calm and positive way. It is not medical advice or a substitute for professional swim instruction.

Always supervise young children around water, stay attentive, and follow guidance from your pediatrician and qualified safety professionals.

Note:
Children with medical conditions, developmental differences, or disabilities may require individualized guidance from their healthcare providers or trained aquatic therapists. Always adapt water experiences to your child's unique needs.

Quick Parent Reassurance
Most pediatric ear infections come from viruses and bacteria, not from clean bath water. Gentle splashing and early tub time are generally safe and developmentally beneficial for most children. If you have specific concerns, your pediatrician can offer personalized guidance.

Important Clarification
The guidance in this book focuses on the misuse of puddle jumpers and similar flotation aids in swimming environments, where they disrupt natural water adaptation and skill development.
We encourage the proper use of Coast Guard–approved life jackets (PFDs) for boating and open-water activities, where they play an essential role in true water safety.

Consider learning CPR and building layers of water safety in and around your home and community.

Your presence, patience, and attention are the foundation of safe water experiences.

www.Prepare2Swim.world

READY GO

by Michael Godleski

THE PUDDLE JUMPER PROBLEM

The widespread normalization — and often the expectation — that children wear puddle jumpers in pools is the foundational error that fuels most of the misinformation in water safety.

It's also a major reason drowning rates haven't improved in decades. And for many parents, the moment their child "moves" in the device creates a powerful illusion of progress — one that often leads them to defend the puddle jumper long after it has begun holding their child back.

A PFD was designed for **boats and open water** — not for pools or learning to swim.

But relentless marketing has recast it as a "teaching tool," reshaping how parents think water safety works.
In a PFD, toddlers laugh, kick, and "swim." They stop clinging. They feel free — and that freedom looks like progress.

But the nervous system doesn't know "pretend swimming." It learns whatever the body repeats.

And a puddle jumper teaches **overexertion** — frantic bicycle kicks, chin-up posture, and shallow, panicked breathing — the opposite of real swimming.

This creates confident beginners with confused bodies — children who feel safe but haven't practiced true balance, breath, or control.
That shows up the moment they enter swim lessons. Instructors spend lesson after lesson *un-teaching* the device's habits and rebuilding calm control from zero.
Meanwhile, younger children — the ones who could thrive with early foundational exposure — get crowded out.

Swim schools stay full reteaching five-year-olds how to start over instead of teaching one-year-olds how to begin right.
Costs rise. Openings shrink. Safety gets delayed instead of developed.
And children continue to enter water boldly and independently — without the healthy hesitation that real experience creates.

This isn't just a pool-toy problem — it's a **cultural one** — built on false confidence, strong marketing, and a misunderstanding of how humans actually learn to swim.

THE KNOWLEDGE GAP

Swimming isn't a trick.

It isn't talent.

And it's never a lightbulb moment.

It's a **neuromuscular adaptation** — the body and brain learning through calm repetition, predictable exposures, and simple patterns repeated over time.

Every splash, float, and breath maps safety into muscle memory.

That's how humans — from four months to forty years — become confident and capable in water.

The earlier this begins, the easier it becomes.

Early exposure prevents fear before it forms.

Comfort becomes instinct — not something to rebuild later.

Children who grow up with calm, consistent water time don't panic when splashed or submerged.

They recognize the sensation.

Their body already knows what to do.

Our goal is simple:

To give them the confidence to be calm in the water — and that **one second of hesitation** that keeps them alive outside of it.

READY GO

Before We Begin...
A Message for the Grown-Ups

At Prepare2Swim, our mission is simple - to save lives through proactive water education, and action.

The journey to safe swimming doesn't start at the pool — *it begins in the bathtub.*

In those first gentle splashes, before your child ever kicks off a pool wall or learns to float, **their relationship with water is quietly taking shape.** These moments aren't just play — **they're powerful.** They lay the foundation for comfort, trust, and body awareness that will stay with your child for a lifetime.

When you pour water calmly over your baby's head, smile through the splashes, and model ease and joy — **you're doing more than preparing for swim lessons.** You're giving them the emotional tools to face water *with confidence, respect, and calm.*

Proactive water education means beginning early — preferably when cleared for water — and using every moment in and around water as an opportunity to build safety, connection, and skill.

It's not just about learning to swim.
It's about how they learn.
And it's about you — the parent, the guide, the calm voice beside them.

As you explore this story together, know this: **you hold the power** to turn everyday water moments — in the bath, at the sink, or in the pool - into meaningful, joyful progress.

The Truth About Drowning — And Why You Can't Wait

Drowning doesn't happen because kids can't swim.

It happens because their brain wasn't built to pause in that moment.

More than 70% of toddler incidents happen when

water isn't even part of the plan —

when conditioning, distraction, opportunity, and ability collide in

one unguarded second.

Drowning is **fast.**

Drowning is **silent.**

Drowning is often missed - even with adults nearby.

The Illusions That Cost Us

We've been misled by things that look safe but aren't.

Floaties give parents confidence, but not children skills.
They create bad posture, **wire the brain** for false support, and delay the journey to real swimming.

Waiting until age 3 or 4 to start "real" lessons.
By then, fear has often taken hold. While we wait, **kids miss hundreds of opportunities** to feel calm and confident in water.

Fun over foundation.
Pool parties with puddle jumpers, **even some lessons**—these create the illusion of safety. But without intentional progress, children become familiar with water... not prepared for it. In panic, that distinction can mean everything.

The Swim-Lesson Landscape

And when parents go looking for lessons, what they find isn't consistent.

Some programs strap kids into chambered flotation devices on day one and promise to "wean" them out later.

Some "swim factories" enroll babies at six months but won't let them submerge until age two.

Some programs use high-pressure methods, hoping stress will force adaptation.

And many children spend months —
sometimes years — in lessons that never align with where their body and nervous system needed to begin.
It's not that these places don't care.
It's that there's no single, proven standard.
— and families are left confused and discouraged.

The Truth

Here's what we've learned after decades in the water:

When a child comes in already comfortable with water on their face, already familiar with breath cues,

already calm on their back —

Any swim school works better.

Early preparation turns lessons into progress, not panic.

Into confidence, not fear.

Into trust, not trauma.

That's why you can't wait.

Because by the time most families realize how important this is, the hardest work has already begun.

About Us: Michael & Dale Godleski

Founders of Prepare2Swim

With a shared passion for water safety, child development, and empowering parents, Michael and Dale Godleski have dedicated their lives to helping families raise confident, capable swimmers-starting from infancy.

Michael Godleski
With 25+ years of hands-on experience, Michael brings unmatched expertise in swimming instruction, movement education, and early childhood development. He holds a degree in Physical Education and Child Development, and his teaching journey includes everything from high school physical education to fourth-grade math and science, to Montessori movement programs for toddlers as young as 18 months.

Michael's approach is rooted in biomechanics, skill development, and smart parenting. Since 1998, he's helped thousands of children learn to swim, not through pressure or fear-but through trust, play, and proven progressions. He believes early water exposure is about more than swimming—it's about lifelong safety, presence, and connection.

Dale Godleski
Dale's swim journey began in 2003, when Michael hired her to help lead large group swim lessons. From teaching toddlers how to float to guiding high schoolers in life skills, Dale has spent years immersed in both education and swim instruction. She holds a degree in Family Consumer Sciences and Child Development and has taught across age groups in both traditional and Montessori environments.

Her decade-plus experience teaching "Mommy & Me" classes, private swim lessons, and working in a competitive swim school gives her a unique ability to meet each family exactly where they are. Dale brings a gentle, nurturing presence, empowering even the most hesitant toddlers-and their parents-to gain confidence in the water.

Together, the Godleskis created Prepare2Swim to give families a clear, loving, and unified proven path to early water acclimation and survival swimming—without relying on floaties, gimmicks, or fear. Their mission is simple:

Trust the child. Teach safety as a way of life. Make water a place of joy, not danger.

What "Prepare2Swim" Really Means

Prepare2Swim isn't just lessons—it's a mindset. A new way families approach water, risk, and readiness.

It means starting early. Teaching the right things in the right order. No floaties, no shortcuts, no one-size-fits-all programs.

To Prepare2Swim means:

- **Readiness**

  Not just physical, but emotional and sensory. From the bathtub to the pool, we build calm confidence step by step.

- **Empowerment**

  Parents lead, kids decide. Families stop outsourcing safety and start owning it—together.

- **Safety**

  We strip away myths (like puddle jumpers "teach" swimming) and replace them with real skills: body control, breath awareness, boundaries.

What It Doesn't Mean

It doesn't mean pushing too early, rushing milestones, or "sink or swim."
It means being present, patient, and prepared.

Because when a family is prepared, a child isn't just safer-they're truly ready to swim.

How to Use This Book

This isn't just a story to read — it's a **tool to begin.** Prepare2Swim was created to help families like yours take water safety into their own hands, starting long before swim lessons. Whether your baby is fresh from the hospital or your toddler is fearful after a bad experience, this book is your gentle push toward confidence - for both you and your child.

Start Early — Really Early
You can begin water acclimation as soon as your baby is home. Use bath time as your classroom: soft splashes, calming language, steady hands. Your tone, presence, and confidence will set the foundation for your child's relationship with water.

Involve the Whole Family
Older siblings can join in, too. Let them model calm behavior in the tub or pool. Water safety becomes a family lifestyle — not a one-time lesson. Build a shared language: *"calm body," "relaxed face," "gentle hands," "walking feet."* These phrases are tools your child will carry with them into the pool and beyond.

Go Slow, Stay Consistent
You don't need to rush. This book is designed for ongoing use — a reminder. The goal is gentle repetition and positive association. Just small steps that build emotional readiness and physical comfort.

This Is Where It Begins
Water safety isn't a milestone you wait for — it's a mindset you create.

This book is your starting point.

Keep it nearby. Read it often. Let it remind you: you're not just reading to your child — you're *preparing them to swim.*

A Message From Us

We started Prepare2Swim because we've seen what happens when children aren't prepared.

After decades of teaching swim lessons and working closely with families, we've seen it all — toddlers too afraid to get in the water, panic, and posture so off-balance it only made things harder. These experiences taught us that most kids don't need more lessons… they need better preparation.

And we've also seen this: one bad moment doesn't have to define a child's relationship with water. What matters most is what happens after. Recovery, reassurance, and returning to play keep the process positive and moving forward.

Real progress starts earlier than most people realize — with simple, intentional steps that build comfort, trust, and confidence in the water from the very beginning.

That's why we built this book — to give parents a way to start now. Gentle. Realistic. Meaningful.

This isn't about pushing your baby to swim overnight. It's about understanding that your calm, confident presence is the greatest tool in water safety.

And yes — that means no floaties.
Floaties create false confidence, bad posture, and a delayed journey. Instead, we slow things down, stay present, and build trust one step at a time.

We believe in early exposure.
We believe in parent-led progress.
And we believe your family can become safer, stronger, and more connected through the water.

Thank you for being here. For choosing a different path. For saying "we're doing P2S." Stay present. Stay playful. Stay safe.

- Michael & Dale Godleski
Founders of Prepare2Swim

From Layla's first "let's film it," to Sloan's early milestones, to Jace,

showing every parent exactly how it's done-

you didn't just inspire this—you built it.

You've held the phone, helped us decide, and changed our family's path.

This story is ours because it's yours.

Love, Mom and Dad

You're here, little one, and we love you more than you'll ever know.

The water will be part of your life - filled with fun, adventure, and memories we'll treasure forever.

Every smile, every splash, every tiny bit of progress is more than play - it's safety, it's confidence, it's protection.

Before the big adventures — splashing, floating, sunny days -

We begin with gentle steps.

Starting early makes the water feel like home: a place of comfort and joy.

With love, intention, and consistency,

Each small step becomes safety, strength, and freedom.

Every swimmer starts small.

It begins with water on your face - gentle drops, playful splashes.

Starting early is the shortcut:

every skill comes quicker, every step smoother,

comfort and confidence growing with every splash.

Let's make it joyful, from the very first one.

Now we'll try something new: a pause.

Not a big breath - just stillness.

Quiet. Calm. No hurry.

We'll whisper, "Reaaddyy... Gooo!"

and let the water fall.

You don't need to "hold" anything -

just wait, let the drizzle pass,

and it's gone.

A tiny pause, a mighty step.

And guess what?

You were born ready for it

The water is ready to hold you, as soon as you let it.

Ears in, body calm, breathing soft —

this is how you'll feel relaxed and protected wherever you swim.

And whenever you need a breath,

we'll remind you: roll to your back.

Here's our plan:

just a **minute or two** of practice during bath time, every few days.

Short and sweet.

Sometimes it will feel like you're leading the way —

but Mom and Dad will always be there to guide you.

When you're in the water, your brothers and sisters will be there too!
We'll all work together in the tub - splashing, laughing, making puddles on the floor.
All that energy, all those cheers, make the water even more fun for you.
And while we play, we're all learning how to help you grow into a swimmer.
This is how our family builds water safety together -
through fun, through words, through love.

Before we begin, we'll gather what we need:

toys, cups for drizzles, towels, diapers, PJs — all within reach.

The tub is clear, the floor is dry, and extra towels wait for your splashes.

Now we're ready to make the water fun, calm, and safe.

Your first tub time is exciting!

Dad is right here with you, making the water just right -

warm and safe around 98 degrees.

Mom is nearby, smiling, while you splash for the very first time.

This isn't just bath time — it's the start of trust, confidence, and independence.

With your ears in the water and your body calm, you'll learn that the water can carry you. Our voices, our songs, our laughter surround you, turning calm into trust, and trust into safety.

We'll look into your eyes, letting you know there's no rush.
You can rest on Mom's or Dad's legs - ears in, toes out, body calm.
Floating begins when you're ready -
when your body is at ease, and your breathing is soft.

For breath-holding, we'll keep it simple and fun -

silly faces, gentle drizzles.

Mom and Dad puff their cheeks like chipmunks.

You might not copy yet - and that's okay.

Someday you will.

Every drizzle, every smile is practice.

And if your mouth stays open, that's okay too -

we'll be right here, close and careful,

until your body finds the rhythm.

Play becomes practice.

Practice becomes safety.

"Reaaddyy... Gooo!"
Dad drizzles water by your ears.
We go slow — just little side drizzles at first.
Clear words. Gentle water. Happy smiles.
Each bath, a little more.
That's how comfort grows.
That's how trust is built.
And when water runs down your face,
we don't rush to wipe it away.
You're learning the water belongs here,
and that it feels just fine.

When drizzles feel easy,
we'll move to little cup pours.
Each splash is a win,
and we'll celebrate every one.
The water feels bigger,
but so does your trust.
Pour by pour, bath by bath,
you're ready for more.
These pours aren't just about water -
they're about timing between us.
The same rhythm we'll use in the pool,
when swimming really begins.

Your first stroke: "Tickle. T. Snap!"

Gentle up. Gentle out. HARD snap down.

This is the start of your motion.

At first, you'll rest on Mom's or Dad's hands,

floating easy on your back.

Each little snap pushes water,

teaching your body how to move.

And when you roll forward to scoop,

your wrists are strong,

your strokes are ready,

and swimming begins.

A tiny cough. A quick blink.
Maybe even a little startle.
That's okay.
It's just you learning what water feels like.

In the tub or in the pool, water can surprise us—even grown-ups.
No rush. No big reaction.
We're right here.

Around 4-6 months, when your head is steady, we'll try your very first swim underwater. Dad holds you snug. He says, "Reaaddyy... Gooo!" And together, we glide.

Smooth.

Gentle.

Easy.

Your first glide isn't a surprise -

it's the next step.

All those drizzles and smiles

have prepared you for this moment.

We smile big.

We clap.

We cheer for you.

Your first glide is a moment to remember.

We're proud, you're proud —

and the whole family feels it too.

Little by little,

splash by splash,

you're becoming a swimmer.

After swim time, we'll lift you out,

cuddle you tight, and slip on your PJs.

This is our favorite part -

the laughter, the snuggles,

the stories we tell about what you did today.

Every practice makes you shine.

And every night ends with love.

This rhythm seals in the joy -

your joy of water, your joy of swimming,

and the ease of learning

Let's keep this going -

little swims, little chats, again and again.

Because water safety isn't just for the tub.

It's a language we grow together -

in the pool, at the beach,

on vacations, at parties,

anywhere there's water.

As you grow, our words will grow too.

Simple cues now.

Bigger conversations later.

Always the same goal:

joy in the water,

and safety that lasts a lifetime.

Dads—

don't be the parent on the sidelines.

Set the tone for this process...

and everything else.

If you found this book a little late,

and your child isn't swimming yet,

there is no scenario where it's not right to get in the water.

Birthday party.

Vacation.

Pool day.

Your child will be proud you're there beside them.

Too many times I've seen kids in puddle jumpers

shouting "Dad, come in!" over and over...

while Dad stays on the phone.

Those moments slip away.

Don't let it get to the point they stop asking.

We only get so much time in this world

with these beautiful little beings.

And the water is where trust is built,

where memories are made,

where love is lived out.

They need you in the water.

They love you in the water - every single time.

Don't let them down.

These moments are precious.

Don't let missed opportunities to strengthen them…

become moments you wish you could get back.

This is who you get to be as their dad.

Your Next Step: Survival Swim Made Simple

This book gives you the foundation - but if you want the complete roadmap, we've built it for you.

The Prepare2Swim Survival Course takes everything in these pages and expands it with step-by-step videos, proven progressions, and the exact strategies we've used to teach thousands of children to swim.

Because you've invested in this book, we're giving you steeply discounted access to the course.

👉Scan the QR code to unlock your discount and start today.

Your Story Matters

Every family's swim journey looks different.
Maybe your baby is just getting comfortable in the tub.
Maybe your four-year-old is learning to glide.
Maybe your child learned that calm comes first — and progress follows.

When this book helps you, pause and notice what changed.
Not just what your child can do — but how they feel in the water.

The confidence. The trust. The ease that replaces hesitation.

Those shifts matter.
They shape how your child relates to water — not just now, but for years to come.
They are the difference between rushing and readiness,
between reacting and staying calm.

And when you think of another parent just starting out —
someone unsure, overwhelmed, or waiting longer than they need to —
share the message forward.

Not because every journey looks the same.
But because starting with calm and intention changes what's possible.

One family beginning this way
can change everything for the family that comes next.

Be Part of the Movement

This book is just the beginning. Every family who starts early is part of a ripple that saves lives. And now that you've taken this step, you can help us make the ripple grow.

How? By sharing.

When you tell another parent about Prepare2Swim, you're not just passing along a book-you're passing along confidence, safety, and peace of mind. And if you want to take it even further, we've built a way for you to join us directly.

The Prepare2Swim Affiliate Program lets families like yours share our courses and resources-and even earn while doing it. It's simple, it's impactful, and it fuels the mission of ending childhood drowning.

Scan the QR code to learn more and see how you can help spread water safety while supporting your own family too.

Together, we can create generations of swimmers who are safer, stronger, and more confident in the water.

- Mike / Prepare2Swim

Continue when You're Ready!

This book gives you the foundation.

If you'd like additional guidance, we've created optional resources that build on what you've learned here — with clear progressions and parent-led video support.

Scan below to explore what's available.

Continue Learning **Help Others Start**

If you're interested in helping other families start with calm and intention,

there's also a way to share this work more directly.

Thank you for being part of the Prepare 2 Swim movement.

www.ingramcontent.com/pod-product-compliance
Lightning Source LLC
LaVergne TN
LVHW070434070526
838199LV00015B/509